**LIFE PROCESSES**

# Survival and Change

Steve Parker

Heinemann Library
Chicago, Illinois

© 2001 Reed Educational & Professional Publishing
Published by Heinemann Library,
an imprint of Reed Educational & Professional Publishing,
100 N. LaSalle, Suite 1010
Chicago, IL 60602

Customer Service  888-454-2279

Visit our website at www.heinemannlibrary.com

Designed by Celia Floyd
Originated by Dot Gradations
Printed by Wing King Tong, in Hong Kong

05 04 03 02 01

10 9 8 7 6 5 4 3 2 1


**Library of Congress Cataloging-in-Pubication Data**

Parker, Steve, 1961-
   Survival and change / Steve Parker.
     p. cm. -- (Life processes)
   Includes bibliographical references (p. ).
   ISBN 1-57572-340-9 (library)
    1. Adaptation (Biology)--Juvenile literature. [1. Adaptation (Biology) 2.
Plants--Habitat. 3. Animals--Habits and behavior. 4. Habitat--Ecology. 5. Ecology.] I.
Title. II. Series.


QH546 .W36 2000
578.4--dc21

                                                             00-057507


**Acknowledgments**
The author and publishers are grateful to the following for permission to reproduce copyright material: Mary Evans Picture Library, p. 28; Natural History Museum London, pp. 23, 26; Natural History Museum London/M. Long, p. 23; NHPA, p. 6; NHPA/A.N.T., p. 13; NHPA/Daryl Balfour, p. 13; NHPA/Anthony Bannister, p. 25; NHPA/A. P. Barnes, p. 7; NHPA/N. A. Callow, p. 28; NHPA/Stephen Dalton, NHPA/Martin Harvey, p. 18; NHPA/Daniel Heuclin, p. 12, p. 19; NHPA/T. Kitchin & V. Hurst, p. 20; NHPA/Stephen Krasemann, p. 9; NHPA/Jean-Louis Le Moigne, pp. 7, 16; NHPA/Trevor McDonald, p. 5; NHPA/Andy Rouse, p. 8; NHPA/Kevin Schafer, p. 22; NHPA/Lady Philippa Scott, p. 11; NHPA/Karl Switak, p. 15; NHPA/M. I. Walker, p. 4; NHPA/David Woodfall, p. 14; NHPA/Norbert Wu, pp. 21, 27; Oxford Scientific Films/Doug Allan, p. 24; Oxford Scientific Films/Rafi Ben-Shahar, p. 15; Oxford Scientific Films/Liz & Tony Bomford, p. 7; Oxford Scientific Films/J. A. L. Cooke, p. 11; Oxford Scientific Films/Konrad Wothe, p. 26; Planet Earth Pictures/Peter Scoones, p. 25.

Cover photograph reproduced with permission of Tony Stone.

Every effort has been made to contact copyright holders of any material reproduced in this book. Any omissions will be rectified in subsequent printings if notice is given to the publisher.

Some words are shown in bold, **like this.** You can find out what they mean by looking in the glossary.

# Contents

## Introduction

More than 4 billion years ago volcanoes poured out red-hot molten rock and choking fumes. No life could survive. By 600 million years ago the warm, shallow seas were filled with worms, jellyfish, and other strange creatures, but there was no life on land. Some 200 million years ago giant dinosaurs pounded through vast forests of firs and pines, but there were no flowers. About 50 million years ago the dinosaurs had all gone, and flowers brightened the landscape. The world and its life have altered greatly in the past. Environmental changes continue today, and animals and plants must **adapt** constantly in order to survive.

# The Distant Past

How do we know about conditions on Earth millions of years ago? Layers of rocks have formed over millions of years. Parts of animals and plants are preserved in these rocks as **fossils.** The animals or plants were buried in sand or mud, which gradually hardened and turned to stone. The hard parts of living things, which did not rot away very quickly after death, formed fossils. They include the teeth, bones, claws, horns, and shells of animals, and the wood, cones, and seeds of plants.

## Change and time

Fossils and other clues show that conditions on Earth have always been changing. During some periods it was warm and damp, with vast steamy swamps. Other times were cold and dry, with massive windy deserts. During great **ice-ages** the land was frozen and snowy. Then there were hot, wet periods with floods and tropical rain forests.

As conditions on Earth changed, living things changed too. They had to cope with the new conditions or risk dying out. This has led to an incredible variety of animals and plants in the past and today. The various ideas about how living things have changed over time to survive and produce the amazing variety of life we have today are explained in this book.

**Fungi,** like this mold, are always ready to decompose dead matter, so the cycle of nature can continue as it has done for millions of years.

## Suited to different places

Conditions around the Earth today vary from mountain peaks to deserts, grasslands, forests, rivers, lakes, beaches, and oceans. Each of these different places is called a **habitat.** Different animals and plants are suited, or **adapted,** to the various habitats.

- The yak has a warm coat of very long, thick fur to keep out the cold in its mountain home, the Himalayas of Asia.
- The limpet has a strong shell and clings strongly to the rocks along beaches to protect itself against crashing waves.
- The deep ocean is very dark and finding food or mates is difficult, so the lantern fish glows to attract its prey or a partner.

The plaice can change its color to blend in with the seafloor so **predators** are less likely to notice it.

## Did you know?

Life may have started more than 3 billion years ago. There are tiny, round objects in certain rocks that could be fossils of the earliest simple, **microscopic** life-forms, and that look like the **bacteria** of today.

# Variety of Life

How many different kinds of living things have you seen today? Perhaps you saw a pet dog or cat, or passed some flowers in the garden or park. You probably saw trees, bushes, grass, and weeds, and birds, butterflies, bees, flies, or worms in the soil. And of course there are the most familiar living things of all—people. To count all of these different kinds of living things would take a very, very long time.

## Species of living things

Scientists around the world are identifying and counting every kind or type of living thing. This will help us study and understand the amazing variety of life on Earth. It will also help us understand how living things have changed over time.

A single kind or type of living thing is called a **species.** All members of a species look very similar to each other and can **breed** or **reproduce** with each other to make more of their kind. But they cannot breed with members of other species. For example, tigers are big cats with striped fur. They are one species of big cats. Lions are similar but have tan fur. They are another, different species. Leopards have spotted fur and are a third species, and so on.

There could be more than 100 different species of **plankton** in a single drop of saltwater.

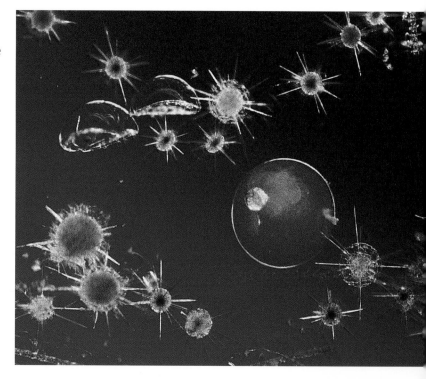

# More and more species

So far, scientists have identified and described more than one and a half million different species. Each species has slight differences from all other species, which make it best suited or **adapted** to survive in its **habitat.** Species on Earth include all kinds of animals and plants, **fungi** like mushrooms, and microscopic life-forms like **amoebas** and **bacteria.** They represent the incredible variety of life, known as **biodiversity.** This variety includes the many different habitats where living things survive, the differences between species, and even **genetic** differences between individuals in a species.

## How many species?

No one knows the total number of species on Earth. They have not all been discovered and counted. There could be 10 million, or 15 million, or perhaps more. New species are described almost every week. Most of these are tiny beetles, weevils, and flies from tropical forests, or worms at the bottom of the sea.

## Did you know?

The largest main group of living things in the world is the insects, with over one million species. And within the insect group, the largest group is the beetles. There are a quarter of a million known species of beetles, but there are probably more. Here are just three beetle species. To show them all would take at least 2,000 books this size.

**Colorado beetle**

**Cockchafer beetle**

**Great diving beetle**

# How Species Differ

There are many kinds of bear. There are grizzly bears in North America, brown bears in Europe, Kamchatkan bears from northeast Asia, and Kodiak bears in Alaska. They vary in size and fur color. But closer scientific study shows that these bears are all very similar. Although they live in different regions in the wild, if they are brought together in parks or zoos, they can **reproduce** with each other. This means they all belong to the same **species.**

The grizzly is one type of the bear species known as the brown bear.

## Geographical differences

The example of the bears shows that they have differences in their **geography,** which means they live in different places. But they all eat very similar foods, make dens in similar ways, raise cubs in the same way, have similar enemies, chiefly humans, and follow very similar life patterns. This means they have very similar **ecology.**

### A ring species

Herring gulls are one example of a **ring species.** The gulls live in a C-shaped ring around the north of the world, with the two ends in Britain. In Britain herring gulls are white, and breed with the herring gulls of eastern America. The American gulls breed with those of Alaska, and the Alaskan gulls breed with those of Siberia. However, the Alaskan and Siberian gulls get progressively smaller with darker markings the farther west you go. At the end of the ring, back in Britain, the herring gulls have become lesser black-backed gulls, which cannot breed with British herring gulls.

## Ecological differences

The opposite is also true. Many kinds of large animals, such as zebras, antelopes, and gazelles, live in the same place, on the African plains. They have the same geography. They

also seem to have the same ecology, since they all eat grass. But closer study shows differences. Zebras tend to eat the longer grass. Wildebeest, also called gnu, feed on medium-length grass leaves. Thomson's gazelles graze on the shortest grasses. These animals avoid **competing** for the same food supply by eating grasses of various lengths.

On the African plains, different large grazing mammals, like zebras and wildebeest, can exist together because they avoid competing for the same food.

## Battle for survival

Two species cannot exist with the same geography and ecology at the same time. They would be direct **competitors** and battle for the same needs, such as food and shelter. One species would soon **adapt** better to the conditions and gradually take over, while the other species died away—unless it changed, too. This battle for survival is the central reason why living things change with time.

### Did you know?
Some species of plants are adapted to growing quickly on bare new land, for example after a fire, earthquake, or volcanic **eruption.** They are called **pioneer species.** They spring up and breed in a short time, spreading seeds far and wide. Gradually, slower-growing plants take over and crowd them out. By then, the pioneer species have reproduced and moved on to new, fresh ground.

# Survival on the Edge

The best conditions for life are year-round warmth, sunshine, and moisture. This is why tropical rain forests are bursting with an incredible **biodiversity** of animals and plants. But what about places on Earth with the worst conditions for life? These include the freezing Arctic **tundra,** the cold blackness of the ocean depths, and sandy, dry deserts where it has not rained for years. Yet even in such severe and extreme conditions, living things find a way to survive.

## Life processes and body chemistry

Every living thing has thousands of natural chemical substances inside its body. These substances are constantly combining together, splitting apart, and undergoing other changes or reactions. These changes are known as body **metabolism,** and are the processes that make up life.

A slight difference in one of the chemical substances may affect metabolism by, for example, allowing a chemical change in the body to happen at a higher temperature. If there is a series of such changes the whole metabolism becomes **adapted** to working at higher temperatures. As this happens the living thing can survive in warmer places, such as the water of a natural hot spring.

## In freezing seas

Ice-fish live in polar seas where the water temperature is below freezing point, 32° Fahrenheit (0° Celsius). The fish do not turn to ice because they have special natural **antifreeze** substances in their blood and body fluids. These substances are similar to the antifreeze chemicals we put into the engines of cars. The chemicals help the ice-fish survive in a **habitat** that would kill other creatures.

# In hot sulphur springs

In natural hot springs water is heated deep in the rocks inside the Earth until it is so hot that it would scald us. But certain **bacterial microbes** such as *Thiobacillus thioxidans* can withstand the temperature. They feed on the sulphur-containing **minerals** dissolved in the water, which are rich in energy and **nutrients**.

**Brine shrimps live in water that is too salty for almost any other living thing.**

## In warm salty water

The ocean contains small amounts of dissolved salt and is home to many living things. But too much salt is very harmful. Salt lakes in **arid** regions are not freshwater, like normal lakes. They have up to ten times the level of salt found in the ocean. Even so, brine shrimps are adapted to live there, and birds come to feed on them.

**Did you know?**
Arabian oryx, a rare type of antelope, live in the baking deserts of the Middle East. In the scorching midday sun their body temperature can rise by 41° Fahrenheit (5° Celcius) without harming them. This increase would kill most other mammals. The oryx cool down again when it gets dark in the evening.

# Unwelcome Guests

A **species** in its original region and **habitat** is part of the balance of nature. Its numbers are kept in check in numerous ways. These include **predators** of many kinds; **competitors** for food, living space, and nest sites; **parasites** such as fleas and lice; various diseases; and severe climate conditions such as a cold winter. Sometimes animals and plants are taken, accidentally or on purpose, to new places that lack these **ecological** checks and controls. The new or **introduced species** can upset the balance in its unnatural home, and can sometimes **breed** out of control to become a very serious pest.

## Spreading around the world

One example of an introduced species is the European or common rabbit. In its original home of southwest Europe and northwest Africa, rabbits are a natural part of the habitat. But in other places, such as Australia, they are very numerous and widespread pests. Rabbits began to spread in Australia in about 1900. Now they eat farm crops, compete with local animals for plant food, take the goodness from the soil and reduce it to dust, and spread diseases.

Why has the rabbit become such a pest? It is an adaptable animal, able to live in a variety of habitats and eat a range of foods. It breeds very quickly. In Australia it has fewer predators than it did in its original home, where its numbers are kept down by foxes, wild cats, stoats, and similar hunters.

The prickly pear, or opuntia cactus, was taken from America to Australia as a hedge plant. But it spread to cover immense areas. Local plant-eating animals could not cope with its sharp spines.

# From pest controller to pest

Sugar cane is a valuable crop in northeast Australia, but sugar cane beetles are serious pests and damage the cane fields. In 1935, one of their natural predators, the cane toad, was brought from South America to Australia to keep the beetles in check. However, this big, powerful, and poisonous toad moved from the cane fields into the surrounding bush. It bred quickly and began to eat the local animals, making some of them rare. Cane toads have now become serious pests themselves.

**The cane toad oozes a poison that may kill an animal that tries to eat it.**

## Controlling numbers

Disease is one form of ecological check or control. Red-knee disease has killed many frogs and similar amphibians in recent years. Whether this is a natural outbreak, or is caused by a human change such as **pollution,** is not clear.

## Did you know?

The water hyacinth is probably the world's worst water-weed. Its natural home is in the tropical waterways of South America. But it has been introduced into Africa and Asia and spread to cover vast areas. Its thick floating masses squeeze out local plants, choke rivers and canals, and prevent boat travel.

**These water hyacinths are taking over the lake in a National Park in Zimbabwe.**

**13**

# Producing Offspring

**Species** stay separate from other species because when their members **breed** or **reproduce,** they produce young of their own species. A mother lion gives birth, not to baby tigers or leopards, but to baby lions. Seeds from a Scotch pine tree grow, not into Corsican pines or Norway pines, but into young Scotch pine trees, like the ones in the picture. This seems very obvious, but how does it happen? How are the features of a living thing passed on from parents to offspring in order to continue the species?

## Instructions for life

Each living thing grows and develops according to a set or list of instructions called **genes.** These are similar to the plans and instructions for building a huge and complex structure such as a jumbo jet or skyscraper. But they are not written on paper! They are in the form of string-like lengths of a chemical known as deoxyribonucleic acid, or **DNA.**

### Built-in behavior

Offspring inherit many features from their parents—including some types of behavior. Ants grow up to look like other ants in their nest. They also carry out jobs such as cleaning, collecting food, and defending the nest, without learning or being taught these tasks. The ants inherit their behavior in the form of genes. This is called **instinctive** behavior.

# Genes in cells

Strings of DNA may be quite long, but they are incredibly thin. They are coiled up tightly inside the microscopic building blocks, or **cells,** that make up all living things. Large living things such as rhinos, trees, and humans have billions of cells. Each cell in a human body contains DNA with more than 100,000 genes. The lengths of DNA from one human cell would stretch almost seven feet (two meters).

**Baby lions receive or inherit certain behaviors, like keeping still when danger is near.**

# Passing on genes

When a female and male of the species breed, they both pass their genes to their offspring. The offspring grow and develop according to these genes. This is why offspring look similar to their parents. The passing on of features or characteristics from parents to offspring, in the form of genes, is known as **heredity.**

### Did you know?

Many living things reproduce when a female and male breed together. This is **sexual reproduction.** But some living things reproduce on their own, without the need for a breeding partner. This is **asexual reproduction.** For example, the creosote bush sends out new stems, which grow their own branches and become new bushes in a ring around the parent. Because the offspring came directly from one parent, they all have exactly the same genes. They are called **clones.**

**The creosote bush reproduces asexually.**

# Everyone Is Different

Have you ever seen a **colony** of seabirds such as gannets? Thousands of birds flap, wheel, soar and dive, calling and squawking to their chicks in the close-packed nests. How do they tell each other apart? They all seem the same. But look closer and there are small differences. Some gannets are bigger than others. Some have slightly longer beaks or slightly wider wings. In fact the gannets are not all the same. They are varied, and in nature even tiny variations are important. They could mean the difference between life and death.

Gannets may look the same, with sharp beaks and gleaming white feathers. But they have slight differences that could affect their survival.

## Similar but not the same

Part of the variation between living things occurs because of their **genes.** In the above example, all of the gannets are from the same **species,** so they have similar genes. But their genes are not exactly the same. There are two reasons for this.

## Mixing genes

First, the genes are not simply passed on as a complete set from parent to offspring. The genes from mother and father are mixed during breeding. Each offspring receives its own unique combination set of genes. It is different from the genes of its mother and father, different from the genes of the other offspring, and different from the genes in every other member of its species. The mixing process that allows this to happen is known as **genetic recombination.**

**16**

# Changing genes

Second, the **DNA** that forms the parent's genes must be copied so it can be passed to the offspring. Sometimes the copying is not exact. The gene is changed or altered, and the offspring receives the new version. This changed gene may have no effect on the offspring. Or it may cause an alteration, such as a difference in size, shape, color, or body chemistry. The change may be helpful or harmful. These changes in a gene are called **genetic mutations.**

## Variety in the garden

Beautiful flowers grow and blossom in the garden. Flowers of the same breed or variety are similar, but they are not exactly the same. Some differences come from their slightly different genes. Others are due to the different conditions where they live. Flowers growing in the shade of a tree may not be as tall and healthy as flowers growing in full sunshine.

Small variations in conditions, such as drier soil or less sunshine, will affect how flowers grow.

## Did you know?

Sometimes living things have exactly the same genes. One example of this is **asexual reproduction.** Another is identical twins. They start as one tiny egg which would normally grow into a single living thing. But the egg divides into two, and then each of these halves goes on to develop into a whole living thing.

# Only Some Survive

As we have seen, two **species** cannot exist with the same **geography** and **ecology** at the same time. One species **adapts** better to the conditions, while the other species dies away or changes. This battle for survival also occurs within a species.

## A world full of boars?

Wild boars live in forests across Europe and Asia. The mother wild boar gives birth to up to ten small, striped boars each year. She may do this from when she starts breeding, at about four years old, until she becomes too old, at perhaps fifteen years. If all wild boar females did this in a few years, wild boars would cover all the land on Earth. But of course, this does not happen, since not all the offspring survive.

Baby wild boar look similar, but the differences between them will determine whether or not they survive.

## The struggle for life

Baby wild boars have many **predators,** so their lives are a struggle for survival. Cats such as leopards and tigers stalk them. Wolves and other wild dogs catch them. Eagles and big hawks can carry them away.

It is not simply luck that determines which babies survive. They are all different, with slightly different **genes.** One boar may have a new feature that gives a slight advantage in survival. This could be a different striped coat pattern for better **camouflage** in the undergrowth, or a stronger **instinct** to stay still and quiet when danger is near.

# Passing on the advantage

The baby boar with the advantage is more likely to survive, grow up, and have offspring of its own. It will pass on its genes, with the new feature, to its offspring. They will also be more likely to survive and **breed** than boars that lack the feature. Gradually, over many generations and thousands of years, the feature will become more common among wild boars. Eventually, all wild boars will have it. Very slightly, the whole species has changed.

## Change by artificial selection

Long ago people captured wild boars and bred together only those that were less fierce, easier to tame, and more likely to produce plenty of meat. Gradually, over thousands of years, this selection by people, known as **artificial selection,** produced modern farm pigs. Other farm animals, from horses and cows to sheep, goats, turkeys, and chickens, have all been bred from wild ancestors by artificial selection.

# Gradual change

This type of change happens not only in wild boars, but in all living things. It is called **evolution.** The species changes or evolves with time, becoming more suited to the conditions as new and better features constantly appear. Change occurs by the process called **natural selection.**

## Did you know?

Some plants eat meat! The Venus flytrap has evolved leaves that can snap closed along the fold in the middle, to trap small creatures such as flies. Then the plant slowly takes in the juices and **nutrients** from the fly's body, to help it grow. Venus flytraps have evolved this feature so that they can live in places where the soil is poor in nutrients, and most other plants cannot grow.

# Change into New Species

Tree shrews are small creatures that look like a combination of shrew and squirrel. But they are not real shrews or squirrels. They are unlike any other mammals and form their own group, called the tupaiids. They live only in the forests of east and south Asia and eat small animals like insects and worms, as well as some seeds and fruits. There are about eighteen **species** of tree shrews. Yet they all look very similar to each other and live similar lifestyles. How did they come about?

## Becoming separate

Imagine one tree shrew species spread across a large forest. During a time of heavy rain, a new river forms, and its waters split the forest into two. Then a volcano **erupts** and forms a mountain barrier, separating the forest into more parts. A huge fire burns, and causes another split in the forest. During a storm some trees are swept down the river, carrying a few tree shrews in their branches. They float across a narrow sea to another forest on a nearby island.

## New species

The single species of tree shrew has been separated in three or four isolated patches of forest. As time passes, conditions in each patch of forest become slightly different. Gradually the tree shrews change too, as they **adapt** by **natural selection** to suit their own surroundings. They cannot **breed** with their relatives in the other patches. Slowly they become different from them. The original single species of tree shrew evolves into a number of new species.

**Different species of tree shrews look similar, as they have probably evolved from one ancestral species.**

# Evolution and diversity

In this way, one species may evolve and split into two or more species. The evidence for this process is all around us; it is why similar species of living things, like the tree shrews, occur in groups or **families** of species. They are similar because they are closely related, having evolved from the same original or ancestor species.

This process of **evolution** into new species has happened countless times, with all kinds of living things, over millions of years, all over the earth. It has given rise to the amazing diversity of life, both in the past and in the world today.

**Did you know?**
Of all species that ever lived on Earth, more than 999 out of 1,000 have now disappeared. Less than 1 in 1,000 are alive today.

# Evolving eels

Garden eels live in burrows on the seafloor. Over long periods of time the sea levels have changed, the water temperature has become colder or warmer, and other conditions have altered. Garden eels in different regions have evolved to suit conditions there, and there are more than 100 different species.

**These garden eels are adapted to the warm waters of the Caribbean.**

## Evolution by natural selection

In 1859, English naturalist Charles Darwin (1809–1882) suggested how evolution happens in his book, *On the Origin of Species*. In the struggle for life, some individuals are better suited or adapted than others. These are more likely to survive, breed, and pass the adaptations to their offspring. It seems that nature itself chooses or selects who lives or dies. Darwin called this idea the theory of evolution by natural selection. It is the theory accepted by nearly all scientists today.

# Prehistoric Life

The process of **evolution** by **natural selection** explains how living things change or evolve over millions of years. It also explains why we find **fossils** of living things that no longer exist. As conditions changed on Earth, new **species** of plants, animals, and other living things appeared. But some species could not cope and died out, or became **extinct.** Others changed or evolved, became better **adapted,** and continued to survive.

## Early forms of life

Fossils suggest that the earliest forms of life on Earth were single **microscopic cells.** However, life-forms gradually became bigger and more complicated. From about 1 billion years ago, seaweeds and soft-bodied animals such as worms and jellyfish began to appear in the seas. This time, between 4.6 billion and 570 million years ago, is called the Precambrian Era.

## Ancient life

At the start of the Paleozoic or "Ancient Life" Era, 570–248 million years ago, the first shelled animals evolved. They included trilobites, ammonites, and brachiopods, or lampshells. Then the first fish appeared in the seas. By 350 million years ago, sharks similar to those of today swam in the oceans. The first small plants grew on land, followed by the first land animals, such as millipedes and insects, then amphibians and reptiles.

**This is a trilobite shell fossil.**

**Did you know?**
Trilobites were ancient cousins of crabs and prawns. However, most of their fossils are not of the whole creatures, but of the shells they cast off or molted.

22

## Middle life

Perhaps the most famous prehistoric animals are dinosaurs. These first walked the land about 230 million years ago, near the start of the Mesozoic, or "Middle Life" Era, 248–65 million years ago. The earliest mammals, small and shrew-like, appeared about the same time. Winged reptiles called pterosaurs flew in the air, and fish-shaped reptiles called ichthyosaurs swam through the seas. The first birds, such as *Archaeopteryx,* also evolved at this time.

**The earliest known bird, *Archaeopteryx,* lived some 150 million years ago.**

## Recent life

At the end of the Mesozoic Era a great change happened, and many kinds of animals and plants disappeared, including dinosaurs, pterosaurs, and ichthyosaurs. This is called a **mass extinction.** The reason may have been a giant block of rock, a meteorite, which smashed into Earth from space. It caused such great and sudden changes that many species could not survive. This marked the beginning of the Cenozoic, or "Recent Life" Era, from 65 million years ago to now. Mammals and birds evolved and became very widespread, as they are today.

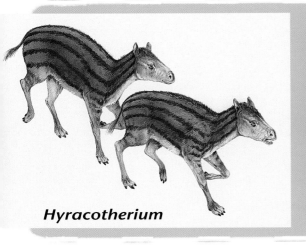

*Hyracotherium*

### Bigger and faster

Fossils through the ages show how horses have evolved to become larger. *Hyracotherium* of 50 million years ago was hardly bigger than a pet rabbit. *Mesohippus* of 30 million years ago was about the size of a large pet dog. The reason for the larger size may have been to run faster and escape from **predators**—since these were also evolving to become bigger.

# Then and Now

**Fossils** in the rocks show that most animals, plants, and other living things have changed or evolved over time. But a few kinds have not. We can see from fossils that some **species** today are similar to living things that lived millions of years ago. These animals and plants are sometimes called "living fossils." How have they survived almost unchanged over such great periods of time?

## Good design the first time

One reason may be that **evolution** produced a living thing that could cope with many conditions, such as different **habitats,** a range of foods, and a variety of **predators.** The adaptable design needed little change through time. Sharks may be an example. They appeared in the seas more than 300 million years ago, and their overall body design is still the same today.

## Stable surroundings

Some types of habitats are very stable. They hardly change with time. So there are few new threats or dangers to cause the living thing to evolve. Fossils show that the lampshells, or brachiopods, were some of the first shelled creatures, appearing in the seas almost 600 million years ago. The mud on the deep ocean floor is much the same now as it was then, and so are the lampshells.

**Lampshells have changed very little in almost 600 million years.**

# Slow evolution

Some living things change quickly, and become very specialized for their habitat and conditions. But as the conditions change again, they are so specialized that they cannot continue to evolve and they die out. However, living things that evolve slowly may be able to cope better with the ever-changing surroundings, through small alterations and adjustments. The velvet worm, or *Peripatus,* is a combination of legless worm and many-legged millipede, with the benefits of each design. Similar worms lived more than 550 million years ago.

The velvet worm still survives among the rotting leaves on the tropical forest floor, as it has done for hundreds of millions of years.

## Did you know?

Scientists thought the fish called the coelacanth died out over 50 million years ago. But in 1938, a living coelacanth was discovered in the Indian Ocean near the Comoros Islands. Since then several more have been found and studied.

## Just lucky?

Fossils of the ginkgo tree, also called the maidenhair tree, go back more than 100 million years. This tree was thought to be **extinct,** but scientists discovered it growing in China. Ginkgoes have now been planted around the world in parks and gardens. The ginkgo could just be a lucky survivor—a species that evolution "forgot."

# The Same but Different

Among the ocean waves, a gray back with a curved fin shows briefly above the surface. At a glance it is not possible to identify the animal properly. It could be a shark. It might be a different type of fish, such as a marlin or swordfish. It may be a dolphin or porpoise, or a young whale. All of these animals are similar in size and in the shape of their back and fin, yet they belong to very different animal groups. Why do they look similar?

## Becoming the same

Moving through water takes much more effort than moving through air. A smooth, streamlined shape makes swimming easier. Many fast water-creatures have a similar body shape, including sharks and other fish, squid, dolphins, porpoises, whales, and even seals and otters. They are long with a pointed front end, a smooth bulge in the middle, and a tapering rear end. They have flaps called fins or flippers to help push them through water and control their movements. These animals are not similar because they are closely related. They have evolved similar body shapes to solve the same problem of swimming fast. This is known as **convergent evolution.**

A dolphin has a smooth, streamlined shape to slip through the water quickly.

An ichthyosaur is an **extinct** type of reptile that lived at the time of the dinosaurs. Its body shape was very similar to the dolphin's.

# Becoming different

The opposite also happens. Living things that were close relatives and had similar body features can gradually become dissimilar. This happens if they live in different places and have different ways of life.

For instance, the fins of the first fish were probably designed for swimming. But **evolution** has produced many other uses for fins. The lionfish has fan-like fins with poison spines for defending itself. The gurnards and tripodfish have spiky walking fins. Mudskippers and climbing perch have fleshy, muscular, arm-like fins to pull themselves along on land. The remora has a sucker-shaped fin on its back to stick to a shark or other large creature, and hitch a ride through the ocean. This is called **divergent evolution.**

## Spines in defense

Desert animals are often desperate for food and water, so they nibble at desert plants. Many very different desert plants have evolved the same defense against being eaten—thorns and spines. They include cacti, euphorbias, and thorn trees, or acacias.

The lionfish's front fins are shaped like sharp spines for jabbing poison at enemies.

The remora's upper fin is shaped like a sucker for clinging to a larger animal, like this shark.

# Survival and Change Today

Until about 10,000 years ago, most of the world was unaffected by people. Then we started to plant crops, keep farm animals, and build villages and towns. The world began to change faster. Now vast areas of once-wild land are used for farming, building, quarrying, mining, roads, parks, and leisure. Humans are changing the world more quickly than ever before. Can animals and plants change fast enough to survive?

## Changing too fast

**Extinction** is a natural part of **evolution**, and it has happened since life began. But today, too many **species** cannot cope with the increased speed of change. Hundreds have died out already. The rate of extinction has increased from around one species every 100 to 1,000 years, to one species every day. The process of evolution by **natural selection** works too slowly for them to **adapt** to the way humans are changing the planet.

## Threats to wildlife

Some animals are killed to make decorative fur coats, or trophies such as horns and tusks. These include elephants, rhinos, and gorillas. Some are killed for no reason other than "sport." Another threat is collection from the wild for the pet and plant trades, which happens to parrots, monkeys, orchids, and cacti. And **pollution** of the air, soil, and water threatens many more species.

About 1,000 years ago, New Zealand was home to the giant moa, a large flightless bird. The moa have all died out— probably hunted to extinction by people.

**28**

# Helping wildlife survive

By far the largest threat to wildlife is **habitat** loss. This occurs when people destroy natural places and change the land for our own use, such as making farms, golf courses, towns, roads, ports, shopping malls, and factories. Wild animals and plants simply have nowhere left to live.

By far the greatest way we can help these threatened species is to slow down, stop, and then reverse the process of habitat loss. We can also reduce the pollution of our surroundings, and our use of rare natural resources, such as hardwood trees. Action is necessary to conserve the beautiful and fascinating variety of wildlife around the world for people in the future.

Bumblebees have become very rare in some regions, because the flowers where they gather their nectar have been sprayed with pesticide chemicals.

## Did you know?

Some types of tourism are harmful to wildlife, such as when people collect living corals. However, some tourism can be helpful. People pay to watch rare animals such as gorillas and whales. They do not disturb the animals, and the money is used to help local wildlife. This is called ecotourism.

## Captive breeding

Some species are so rare that their only hope may be captive breeding. The animals are brought to wildlife reserves, parks, or zoos where they **breed.** Their offspring are then carefully put back into suitable wild places. This captive breeding has been tried for several species, such as golden lion tamarins, California condors, Arabian oryx, and Przewalski's horses.

# Glossary

**adapt, adaptation** change in a feature of a living thing that helps it to fit into its surroundings, or environment, and improve its chances of survival

**amoeba** tiny single-celled organism

**antifreeze** chemical substance that does not freeze solid when it becomes very cold

**arid** hot and dry, like a desert

**artificial selection** when people, rather than the forces of nature, choose which living things survive and breed

**asexual reproduction** when something creates new individuals from a single parent dividing in two

**bacteria** living thing, only visible under a microscope, and found almost everywhere on Earth

**biodiversity** range or variety of living things in a place

**breed** to have babies

**camouflage** blending in with the surroundings, usually by shape, color or pattern, to be less noticeable

**clone** identical living thing that has exactly the same genes as its parent

**competing** struggling for the same food or shelter

**competitor** living thing that tries to obtain the same substance or requirement as another, such as food, shelter, or a place to nest

**convergent evolution** when different living things change so that they appear to be similar, usually because they have similar lifestyles

**divergent evolution** when similar living things change so that they become different, usually because they have lifestyles that are different from each other

**DNA** deoxyribonucleic acid, a chemical substance in living things that carries information in the form of genes

**ecology, ecological** how animals, plants, and other living things survive together in their surroundings

**eruption** when a volcano spurts out fumes, ash, and red-hot, molten rock or lava

**evolution** when living things change or alter—evolve—over time

**extinct, extinction** when every member of a group or species has died, so that the group or species no longer exists

**family** in nature, a group of similar kinds or species of living things

**fossils** remains of once-living things that have been buried and turned to stone in layers of rock

**fungi** large kingdom of living things that obtain energy by decaying or decomposing other living things

**gene** information in the form of a body chemical, DNA, that carries the instructions for a living thing to develop and survive

**genetic mutation** when genes change due to an alteration in the chemical code of their DNA

**genetic recombination** when genes are mixed and come together in new, different groupings or combinations

**30**

**geography** features of the earth's surface, such as mountains, rivers, and seas

**habitat** distinctive type of place or surroundings, such as a woodland, mountain top, grassland, pond, or seashore

**heredity** process of passing genes and characteristics from parent to offspring

**Ice Age** very cold time in Earth's history, when snow and ice covered much more land and sea than today

**instinct, instinctive** when an animal has the information about how to carry out an action in its genes, without having to learn it

**introduced species** kind of animal or plant that is taken to a new region where it does not naturally occur

**mass extinction** when many species of living things die out at about the same time

**metabolism** changes that occur in the chemicals and other substances inside the body of a living thing

**microbe** tiny microorganism, like bacteria, that can only be seen under the microscope

**mineral** substance that helps build your body and keep it healthy

**natural selection** when the forces of nature, such as severe weather or lack of food, affect which living things survive and breed

**nutrient** substance needed by a living thing for its growth, development, and survival

**parasite** plant or animal that lives on or in other plants or animals and gets all its food from them

**pioneer species** one of the first or earliest species in a new or strange place

**plankton** tiny plants and animals that live in the water and provide food for many other animals

**pollution** when unnatural and harmful substances or chemicals collect in a place, harming or interfering with life there

**predator** animal that hunts and kills other animals for food

**reproduce** when a living thing breeds or makes more of its own kind

**ring species** species that alters gradually across a wide area where it lives, so that in some places its members look different

**sexual reproduction** creation of new individuals that requires both a male and a female parent

**species** group of living things that look similar to each other and can breed together, but that cannot breed with other living things

**tundra** flat, treeless region in a very cold place, where the soil is frozen solid for part of the year

# More Books to Read

Fullick, Ann. *Charles Darwin*. Chicago, Ill.: Heinemann Library, 2000.

Fulvio, Cerfolli. *Adapting to the Environment*. Austin, Tex.: Raintree Steck-Vaughn Publishers, 1999.

Llamas, Andreu. *Mammals Dominate the Earth*. Broomall, Pa.: Chelsea House Publishers, 1996.

Snedden, Robert. *Life*. Broomall, Pa.: Chelsea House Publishers, 1995.

# Index